COMPUTERIZED ACCOUNTING

using **QUICKBOOKS PRO 2012**

2ND EDITION

Student Problems & Cases

Alvin A. Arens, D. Dewey Ward, and Carol J. Borsum

Images used on the front cover and throughout this book were obtained under license from Dreamstime.com and Shutterstock.com.

© 2012
Copyright by Armond Dalton Publishers, Inc.
Okemos, Michigan

"QuickBooks Pro" is a registered trademark of Intuit Software in the United States and/or other countries and is used by Armond Dalton Publishers, Inc. under license from owner. *Computerized Accounting Using QuickBooks Pro 2012* is an independent publication not affiliated with Intuit Software.

ISBN 978-0-912503-39-4
Printed in the United States of America

Student Problems & Cases

TABLE OF CONTENTS

Preparation For Question Pages

This book contains questions dealing with material in the Instructions book. Answer all questions in the answer spaces provided below each question. Note that all pages in this book are on perforated pages to enable you to tear out the question/problem pages and hand them in to your instructor. It will be more convenient if you tear out all question/problem pages for each chapter as you go. Be sure to write your name in the space provided at the top of each question/problem page before handing it in.

Some of the chapters in this project include problems as well as questions. While questions usually require only a written answer in the spaces provided, problems often include printouts of solution material from the software. Be sure to include your name and the problem number on all question/problem pages and printouts that you hand in to the instructor.

Because of practice exercises and chapter problems as you work with the Instructions book, each of you may have different transactions and balances in the company data sets used in those exercises. It is important that you start the problem material for each chapter with clean versions of the sample companies. In order to ensure this, before you start the problem material for each chapter you will need to restore both Rock Castle Construction and Larry's Landscaping & Garden Supply data sets from the initial backups that you were asked to copy from your CD to your hard drive in Chapter 1 of the Instructions book. Refer to Chapter 1 for information about the initial backups and restoring the backed up data sets. After restoring both companies, you can then proceed to the problem material for each chapter.

This page is intentionally blank.

Name:

Questions About Familiarization

As described on page v of this book, you should restore both Rock Castle Construction and Larry's Landscaping & Garden Supply using the initial backups you copied to your hard drive while completing Chapter 1. Restore both companies before working on this chapter's problem material.

Question 2-1. Changing companies

 Open QuickBooks and Larry's Landscaping & Garden Supply. Then, switch from Larry's Landscaping & Garden Supply to Rock Castle Construction.

Required

List the steps you followed to change companies from Larry's Landscaping & Garden Supply to Rock Castle Construction.

_____

_____

_____

_____

_____

_____

Name:

Question 2-2. Transaction cycles

Required

List the three transaction cycles you will be using in these materials.

_____

_____

_____

Question 2-3. Menu bar and Icon bar

a. What is the difference between the Menu bar and Icon bar, and where is each located?

_____

_____

_____

_____

_____

b. Which Menu bar item is used the most in these materials?

_____

Question 2-4. Icon bar activities

Required

a. What is the purpose of the Icon bar?

_____

_____

b. Which Icon bar icon is used most extensively in these materials?

_____

Name:

Question 2-5. Home Page

Required

a. How is the Home Page accessed?

_____

b. What is the Home Page used for?

_____

_____

c. Name the three vertical icons and the purpose for each.

_____

_____

_____

Question 2-6. Vendor Center

Required

a. Identify three ways to open the Vendor Center.

_____

_____

_____

b. Assume you want to change the payment terms for a vendor. Which tab in the Vendor Center will you use?

_____

c. List the steps you would follow to change the vendor's payment terms.

_____

_____

_____

Name:

Question 2-7. Vendor Center activities

Required

For each of the following activities in the Vendor Center, state the tab, item on a list, or icon you will use to perform the activity. In some cases you will need more than one of these.

a. Perform maintenance for a new vendor.

b. Print the list of all active vendors, including the account balance due.

c. Prepare a list of all purchase orders for a period of time without printing the list.

d. Export to Excel a list of all bills paid for a period of time.

Question 2-8. Home Page icons

Required

For each of the following activities, identify the icon that is used to open the relevant window.

a. Record a cash sale to a customer.

_____

b. Receive inventory with a bill from the vendor.

_____

c. Pay employees by check.

_____

d. Issue a credit memo to a customer for returned goods.

_____

e. Record a cash receipt from a customer for an outstanding sales invoice.

_____

f. Write a check to a vendor for an expense that has not been recorded as an account payable.

_____

Name:

Question 2-9. Print or not print a document

✧ *Click the Create Invoices icon on the Home Page and examine the window that is opened to determine if there is a print icon.* Is there a print icon?

_____

✧ *Click the Enter Bills icon on the Home Page and examine the window that is opened to determine if there is a print icon.* Is there a print icon?

_____

Required

Explain why there is a print icon on one of the windows and not the other.

_____

_____

_____

_____

Question 2-10. Differences in *QuickBooks* terms

Required

Explain the difference between the following:

a. Home icon and Home Page

_____

_____

_____

_____

Name:

b. Maintenance and processing information

_____

_____

_____

_____

_____

c. Menu bar and Icon bar

_____

_____

_____

_____

_____

d. Vendor Center and Employee Center

_____

_____

_____

_____

_____

Name:

Question 2-11. Default information

Required

a. Briefly explain what is meant by default information.

_____

_____

b. What is the purpose of having default information in *QuickBooks*?

_____

_____

Question 2-12. Name and purpose of *QuickBooks* buttons and icons

State the name and purpose of each of the following buttons or icons:

	Name	Purpose
☑	Check box	
◉	Radio button	
▼	Drop-down list arrow	
▦	Date button	
☐	Text box	
Export	Export button	
🖨	Print icon	

Name:

Question 2-13. Finding information in *QuickBooks*

An important feature of any software package is the degree of "user friendliness" that the software has built in to help new users understand the software more easily. *QuickBooks* has a substantial amount of such "user friendliness." These questions exercise your ability to find relevant information that may or may not have been discussed thoroughly in the chapter.

Required

a. What is the date and amount of the last sales invoice for Ecker Design, a customer of Larry's Landscaping & Garden Supply?

_____

b. Shane Hamby works for Larry's Landscaping & Garden Supply. What is his social security number?

_____

c. Which Larry's Landscaping & Garden Supply customer owes the company the most money, and what is the total amount owed?

_____

d. Which company, Rock Castle Construction or Larry's Landscaping & Garden Supply, has the most Year-to-Date Gross Profit and Net Income?

_____

e. As of 12/31/2016, how much in total dollars did Rock Castle Construction have of receivables delinquent between 31–60 days and over 90 days? (*Hint:* After changing the date to 12/31/2016, click the Refresh button.)

_____

_____

Name:

Questions About Maintenance

As described on page v of this book, you should restore both Rock Castle Construction and Larry's Landscaping & Garden Supply using the initial backups you copied to your hard drive while completing Chapter 1. Restore both companies before working on this chapter's problem material.

QUESTION 3-1. Waren Sports Supply

Required

a. What is the credit limit for the customer Clayborn University?

b. If you wanted to change the credit limit, how would you do it?

c. What is the street address for the employee Jim Adams?

d. Why do you believe there is no address or credit limit for the customer CASHCUSTOMER?

e. What is the selling price and cost for the inventory item BB-019 basketball pole pad?

Name:

QUESTION 3-2. Rock Castle Construction

Required

a. What are the Terms and Tax Item for a credit to sales for a sale to the customer Bauman, Mark?

b. Attempt to delete the 2nd story addition job for the customer Cook, Brian. What is the message when you attempt to delete it?

c. Why do you believe there is a control preventing you from deleting this customer?

d. Explain why you must be sure you want to delete any account before you do so.

e. How many general ledger subaccounts for the expense account #60100 Automobile does Rock Castle Construction have?

f. Add the following general ledger account. (*Hint:* Type the information and press [Enter] or use the drop-down lists when available to select the correct information.)

▧	**Account Type:**	Accounts Receivable
▧	**Number:**	11300
▧	**Account Name and Description:**	Receivable from Management

How many entries did you type and how many did you select using the drop-down list?

_____

g. Attempt to delete the record that you added in Question 3-2f. Were you able to delete it?

_____

h. What is the current annual salary amount for Dan T. Miller? (*Hint:* After you open the Edit Employee window for Miller, select Payroll and Compensation Info in the Change tabs drop-down list.)

_____

i. Change the annual salary amount to $43,000.00 and save the changes. After the change, reopen his employee record and view the salary amount. Is it the same as the one you entered when you changed it? Explain what happened.

_____

_____

j. Explain why it is essential for companies to have controls dealing with access to the *QuickBooks* software.

_____

_____

Name:

Questions About Transaction Processing

QUESTION 3-3. Overview of processing information

Required

a. Explain the difference between maintenance and processing transactions for the sales and cash receipts cycle. Which of the two is done first?

_____

_____

_____

_____

_____

_____

b. Which of the following activities involves transaction processing in the sales and collection cycle?

1. Receive a customer payment
2. Adding a new customer
3. Purchasing inventory
4. Billing customers
5. Preparing a payroll check
6. Entering the date of a cash sale
7. Printing an invoice

_____

_____

_____

_____

_____

Name:

c. Assume you have just opened a company and want to begin processing transactions. In the table below, identify which transaction cycle and which icon on the Home Page you will select to process each of the transaction types. The first row is provided as an example.

Transaction Type	Accounting Cycle	Home Page Icon Button
Prepare a sales invoice	Sales & Cash Receipts	Create Invoices
Deposit today's receipts		
Receive inventory		
Record employee's time worked		
Order new inventory		
Issue credit for returned goods on a sale		

Name:

QUESTION 3-4. Examining sales invoices for Rock Castle Construction

Required

a. What is the total amount of Invoice No. 1071 for Pretell Real Estate—155 Wilks Blvd. and what is the balance due on that invoice?

b. Describe the service provided to Pretell Real Estate for the invoice.

c. What type of items on the invoice are taxable in San Domingo County and which are non taxable?

d. What amount will be credited to sales for the transaction?

QUESTION 3-5. Processing sales invoices for Larry's Landscaping & Garden Supply

Required

    a. Assuming Larry's Landscaping & Garden Supply wants to issue sales invoices numbers sequentially, what should the next invoice number be? How did you determine this?

_____

_____

Process Sales Invoice No. 142 on Purchase Order 3749 for the sale of the following items on 12/16/2016 to E. Benjamin Cheknis:

        ▨ *6 hours of tree & shrub trimming.*
        ▨ *8 Hedges & Shrubs.*
        ▨ *4 hours of Installation of landscape design.*

    b. What is the source of information *QuickBooks* uses for the selling price for these three items?

_____

    c. What document is the person processing sales invoice transactions likely to use to obtain the customer name and type of services desired by the customer?

_____

    d. What is the total amount due on the invoice and what part of that is applied to sales? What makes up the difference?

_____

_____

    e. Print the sales invoice. What else do you need to do to save the invoice before exiting?

_____

_____

Name:

QUESTION 3-6. Additional processing of sales invoices for Larry's Landscaping & Garden Supply

Required

This question continues with additional parts following up on what you did in Question 3-5.

✧ *In addition to the items that you have already recorded, add the following two items to Invoice No. 142: 2 Citrus Tree–50 gal and 2 additional hours of Installation of landscape design.*

✧ *Prepare the revised invoice and save it.*

    a. Explain how you prepared the revised sales invoice.

    b. What is the total amount of the revised invoice?

✧ *Void Invoice No. 142.*

    c. How is Invoice No. 142 included in the Invoices List?

    d. What is the amount due on Invoice No. 142 now?

Name:

QUESTION 3-7. Maintenance and processing of sales invoices for Larry's Landscaping & Garden Supply

Change the unit selling price for the non-inventory item Citrus Tree–50 gal from $66.00 to $660.00.

Process Sales Invoice No. 143 on purchase order 49687 for the sale of 5 Citrus Tree–50 gal to Craig Crider on 12/20/2016. Do not save the invoice yet.

a. What is the total invoice amount for Invoice No. 143? Why is the invoice amount for this invoice more than the entire amount for invoice No. 142 even though fewer items were sold?

_____

_____

_____

b. What, if anything, can management do to control accidental or fraudulent changes in unit selling prices?

_____

_____

_____

c. Print Sales Invoice No. 143 and turn it in to your instructor.

QUESTION 3-8. Deleting a transaction for Larry's Landscaping & Garden Supply

a. Examine the list of sales invoices on the Customer Center: Invoices. Why is Invoice No. 143 included even though it was not saved in Question 3-7?

_____

_____

Delete Invoice No. 143 and look at the Customer Center: Invoices again.

b. Is Invoice No. 143 included?

_____

Name:

Questions About Internal Controls

QUESTION 3-9. Question about automatic entry controls for Larry's Landscaping & Garden Supply

Required

a. What is meant by automatic entry controls and what are their purposes?

_____

_____

_____

_____

_____

_____

Click the Enter Bills icon on the Home Page to open the Enter Bills window. Before selecting a vendor, look carefully at the window. Now select Brown Equipment Rental.

b. List the entry box and automatic entry control entries that resulted from selecting the vendor name before any additional information is entered.

_____

_____

_____

_____

_____

Name:

QUESTION 3-10. Question about automatic calculation and posting controls for Rock Castle Construction

Required

a. What is meant by automatic calculation and posting controls and what are their purposes?

_____

_____

_____

_____

_____

❖ *Open the Enter Bills window and select the Items tab. Enter the following for the vendor Custom Kitchens of Bayshore:*

   ▪ *Cabinets – Light Pine for Item and 4 for Qty.*
   ▪ *Hardware – Lk Doorknobs for Item and 10 for Qty.*

b. Identify the automatic entry and calculation controls shown on the window that resulted from the previous entries. Which were automatic calculation controls and which were automatic entry controls?

_____

_____

_____

_____

_____

_____

_____

Name:

c. What would the accounting entry (debit and credit) have been for the transaction if you had saved it?

_____

_____

_____

d. Identify three purchase records that would have been automatically updated as a result of the entry in Question 3-10b if you had saved the transaction.

_____

_____

_____

_____

e. Identify four non-purchase records that would have been automatically updated as a result of the entry in Question 3-10b if you had saved the transaction.

_____

_____

_____

_____

_____

Cancel the transaction that you just entered.

Name:

QUESTION 3-11. Question about complete data controls for Rock Castle Construction

a. What is meant by complete data controls and what are their purposes?

_____

_____

_____

_____

b. What two boxes in an Enter Bills window must have information included for *QuickBooks* to accept the transaction? What message is provided for each if the information is missing?

_____

_____

_____

_____

_____

_____

c. Assume you enter information in the two boxes in Question 3-11b, but not in any other boxes, and then save the transaction. Will the transaction be recorded? If so, what is the effect on the financial statements? (*Hint:* Process and save a transaction with only the two required boxes filled. Then examine the Bills List. If it is included, you should delete it when you have completed answering Question 3-11c.)

_____

_____

_____

_____

Name:

QUESTION 3-12. Question about valid data controls for Rock Castle Construction

    a. What is meant by valid data controls and what are their purposes?

_____

_____

_____

_____

_____

    b. Open the Enter Bills window and start recording a bill from Cal Telephone. Make up details for recording the transaction, including invalid data. Give two examples of the invalid data you attempted to enter and the resulting valid data control messages generated by *QuickBooks*.

_____

_____

_____

_____

_____

_____

_____

_____

Name:

Questions About Lists

As described on page v of this book, you should restore both Rock Castle Construction and Larry's Landscaping & Garden Supply using the initial backups you copied to your hard drive while completing Chapter 1. Restore both companies before working on this chapter's problem material.

QUESTION 4-1. Rock Castle Construction — Questions about customers, sales, and collections

Required

a. Which customer has the largest outstanding account balance on the current date (12/15/2016)? Which one has the smallest balance excluding zero balances?

b. What is the total amount of invoices for the current fiscal year-to-date? *Hint:* Enter the proper time period in the Date box.

c. What is the total amount of open invoices for the current month to date (12/1/2016 to 12/15/2016)?

d. Which customer paid the largest amount using MasterCard this fiscal year-to-date?

Name:

QUESTION 4-2. Rock Castle Construction — Questions about payroll

Required

a. How many paychecks did Elizabeth Mason receive in November 2016?

_____

b. Explain the difference between the nature of payroll checks and liability checks for payroll.

_____

_____

_____

_____

_____

_____

_____

_____

c. Which employee received the largest net paycheck every pay period in the current fiscal year?

_____

QUESTION 4-3. Rock Castle Construction — Print a list of payroll checks

Required

Print a list of payroll checks for the third quarter of 2016 (7/01/16 to 9/30/16), sorted by net pay from largest to smallest. The list should include the following columns from left to right: employee name (Employee), net pay (Amount), date, and paid through.

Name:

Question About Export

QUESTION 4-4. Rock Castle Construction — Print a list of vendors' transactions and export the list

Required

a. Print a list of bills for the vendor Perry Windows & Doors for the current fiscal year to date using only four columns in the following order from left to right: Amount, Open Balance, Date, and Due Date. Sort the list by account balance, with the largest amount on top. *Hint:* Start with the Vendor Center and Vendors tab open so that you can segregate Perry Windows & Doors' transactions.

b. Export the list in part a to Excel using the Export Transactions menu item. After exporting to Excel, print a list of bills for Perry Windows & Doors with an invoice amount of $1,000 or more. Except for the excluded bills, the columns and sorting should be the same as in Question 4-4a. All headings should be in bold. The printout should include a description of the printout and the date.

Name:

Questions About Drill Down

QUESTION 4-5. Larry's Landscaping & Garden Supply — Use drill down in cash receipts

Required

 Open the Customer Center: Received Payments list window.
Drill down on Check No. 3250 dated 11/20/2016.

a. Who was the customer?

b. Were there any other sales to the customer in Question 4-5a that are currently unpaid? Explain.

c. What was the sales invoice number and date of the sale for the above collection?

d. What products or services were sold on the invoice?

e. Was a discount taken by the customer on this receipt?

Name:

QUESTION 4-6. Larry's Landscaping & Garden Supply — Use drill down of employees

Required

Open the Employees Center and use drill down to open the Edit Employee window for Shane Hamby.

a. What is his social security number?

_____

b. What is his annual salary amount?

_____

c. What is his filing status for federal taxes?

_____

d. For the payment to Hamby on 6/16/2016, what was the amount of his total earnings and federal income tax withholding?

_____

_____

e. How much did Larry's Landscaping & Garden Supply pay for his Federal unemployment for the pay period 6/16/2016?

_____

f. How much was the total year-to-date California withholding on this paycheck (year-to-date through 6/16/2016)?

_____

Name:

QUESTION 4-7. Larry's Landscaping & Garden Supply — Use drill down of Chart of Accounts

a. Use drill down to determine the balance in the Bank of Anycity Loan account at 11/30/2016. What is the balance?

_____

b. What were the total debits and credits for the 10/28/2016 transaction to that account?

_____

_____

_____

_____

_____

Name:

Questions About Custom Transaction Detail Reports

QUESTION 4-8. Larry's Landscaping & Garden Supply — Custom Transaction Detail Report for service transactions

Management wants a listing of all invoice transactions in November 2016 in excess of $500.

Required

a. Prepare and print the report.

b. What services were provided for the invoice with the largest invoice amount?

_____

_____

_____

QUESTION 4-9. Larry's Landscaping & Garden Supply — Custom Transaction Detail Report for pest control

Management is considering eliminating a non-inventory item, Ornamental (Plants/Trees), because the revenue generated is less than the costs of providing the services.

Required

What were the total sales of Ornamental (Plants/Trees) last fiscal year? *Hint:* Use Item for the Filter.

_____

_____

Name:

Requirements For Reports

REQUIREMENT 4-1. Larry's Landscaping & Garden Supply — Print a profit & loss statement

Required

a. Print and hand in a standard profit and loss statement for Larry's Landscaping & Garden Supply for this fiscal quarter to date (10/01/2016 to 12/15/2016) in two columns.

b. Print and hand in a standard profit and loss statement for Larry's Landscaping & Garden Supply, by quarter, for the last fiscal year. Each quarter and the total should be in separate columns.

c. Which quarter was the most profitable for the company during the last fiscal year?

REQUIREMENT 4-2. Rock Castle Construction — Print a sales report and use drill down

Required

a. Print and hand in the Sales by Customer Summary Report for Rock Castle Construction for the current fiscal year.

b. Using only drill down, access Invoice No. 1040 for Sonya Bristol and print the sales invoice.

REQUIREMENT 4-3. Rock Castle Construction — Print an accounts receivable aging summary

Required

a. Print and hand in the aged accounts receivable aging summary for Rock Castle Construction as of December 15, 2016. Use interval days of 10 through 40 days past due.

b. Print and hand in the aged receivables for Hendro Riyadi as of December 15, 2016.

Name:

REQUIREMENT 4-4. Larry's Landscaping & Garden Supply — Print a general ledger trial balance and export it to Excel

Required

a. Print and hand in the general ledger trial balance for Larry's Landscaping & Garden Supply as of October 31, 2016.

b. Export to Excel the general ledger trial balance for Larry's Landscaping & Garden Supply as of October 31, 2016. Then delete all accounts except income statement accounts. Print and hand in the report.

c. Print and hand in the general ledger trial balance for Larry's Landscaping & Garden Supply as of October 31, 2016, for income statement accounts only, but including retained earnings, using *QuickBooks* instead of exporting to Excel. *Hint:* Use modify Reports.

d. Which approach in Requirements 4-4b or 4-4c do you prefer? Why?

_____

_____

_____

_____

e. Print and hand in the general ledger trial balance as of June 30, 2016, for the following accounts: all cash accounts, all fixed asset accounts, all accumulated depreciation accounts, and all equity accounts.

f. Explain how you accomplished Requirement 4-4e.

_____

_____

_____

_____

Name:

Problems Dealing With the Purchases and Cash Disbursements Cycle

As described on page v of this book, you should restore both Rock Castle Construction and Larry's Landscaping & Garden Supply using the initial backups you created in Chapter 1 before working on this chapter's problem material.

PROBLEM 6-1. Larry's Landscaping & Garden Supply — Purchase Orders

Required

a. How many purchase orders have been processed so far in the current fiscal quarter (10/01/2016–12/31/2016)?

_____

b. What is the amount of the two largest purchase orders for the current quarter (10/01/2016–12/31/2016)?

_____

_____

c. How many different products were ordered on the largest purchase order for the last fiscal year?

_____

_____

_____

d. For Purchase Order No. 4, what was the unit cost of the inventory for the item purchased?

_____

e. Examine Purchase Order No. 4. Where was the inventory item shipped?

_____

_____

_____

f. What accounts are debited and credited when a purchase order is processed?

_____

_____

PROBLEM 6-2. Rock Castle Construction — Purchases

Required

a. How many purchases did Rock Castle Construction make this week (12/11/2016–12/17/2016) through the Bills process? (Do not include credits.)

_____

b. How many of those purchases are not fully paid as of 12/17/2016?

_____

c. What is the amount of the largest purchase so far in 2016 (this fiscal year) through the Bills process and who is the vendor?

_____

_____

d. How many different products were purchased from McClain Appliances on Invoice No. 954592, and what was the total amount of the purchase?

_____

_____

Name:

e. How can you determine if the purchase in Problem 6-2d had been purchased with a purchase order or without one?

_____

_____

f. What are the differences in the quantity and total amount of the inventory ordered versus the quantity and total amount received on the McClain Appliances Invoice No. 954592?

_____

_____

g. What is the total amount of purchases through the Bills process so far in 2016, including credits and the amount of the unpaid purchases?

_____

_____

_____

h. What is the smallest open balance other than 0 at 12/15/2016 (this fiscal year-to-date)?

_____

_____

_____

i. What general ledger accounts are debited and credited when Bills are entered?

_____

_____

_____

_____

Name:

j. What is the total amount of purchases (Bills process) for October and November 2016 combined? *Hint:* Export to Excel and obtain the information.

_____

PROBLEM 6-3. Rock Castle Construction — Cash Disbursements

Required

a. Describe the difference between Bill Payments and Checks in *QuickBooks*.

_____
_____
_____
_____

b. What are the accounting debits and credits when transactions are processed using Bill Payments?

_____
_____
_____
_____

c. What are the accounting debits and credits when transactions are processed using Checks?

_____
_____
_____
_____

d. What was the total of cash disbursements through Bill Payments for the fiscal year-to-date ended 12/31/2016? What was the amount of the largest disbursement in September 2016?

_____

_____

e. Was Check No. 286 for the purchase of inventory or something else? How did you determine this?

_____

_____

_____

_____

_____

f. Answer the following questions for the payment to McClain Appliances in the amount of $3,828.70 on Check No. 366 (in Bill Payments).

  ▪ What was the invoice number for the purchase and the date the inventory was received?

_____

_____

  ▪ What were the discount terms of the purchase?

_____

  ▪ What was the purchase order number for the purchase and the date of the purchase order?

_____

_____

■ Did Rock Castle Construction take the discount and was it appropriate for them to do so?

_____

_____

■ Did Rock Castle Construction receive all of the inventory that was ordered?

_____

_____

g. How many cash accounts were used to record cash disbursements during the current fiscal year?

_____

_____

h. How many cash disbursement transactions in November 2016 were recorded without having been previously recorded as an accounts payable and what was the largest amount?

_____

_____

i. What were the account numbers debited and credited for Check No. 425?

_____

_____

_____

_____

Name:

PROBLEM 6-4. Larry's Landscaping & Garden Supply — Accounts payable

Required

a. What is the total accounts payable on 12/15/2016? How did you determine that information?

_____

_____

_____

_____

_____

b. Which vendor has the largest outstanding balance?

_____

_____

PROBLEM 6-5. Rock Castle Construction — Vendors

Management wants a list of vendors with account balances sorted from the largest to the smallest amount outstanding. The following columns are to be included, from left to right: active status, vendor name, balance payable, type of vendor, and terms.

Required

Prepare and print the list requested by management.

Name:

PROBLEM 6-6. Rock Castle Construction — Purchases, disbursements, and accounts payable

Required

You know that beginning accounts payable, plus purchases on account, minus purchases returns and allowances, minus payments on account equals ending accounts payable. Show that reconciliation by using the information available in *QuickBooks* for November 30, 2016, and beginning and ending accounts payable.

PROBLEM 6-7. Rock Castle Construction — Purchases

The management of Rock Castle Construction wants a listing of all purchases in excess of $750 for October and November 2016. The listing is to be sorted by purchase invoice total from largest to smallest amount and is to include only the following four columns in the order listed, from left to right: vendor name, invoice total, outstanding balance at 12/15/2016, and invoice date. The listing should include a total of the invoice amounts.

Required

Prepare and print the list in the format requested by management. Export to Excel if it is necessary to prepare the report.

Name:

PROBLEM 6-8. Rock Castle Construction — Accounting transactions resulting from processing purchasing and cash disbursement transactions

For each of the following transactions write the debit(s) and credit(s) to the general ledger for Rock Castle Construction including the account number(s). Leave any DR or CR blank if no account number is affected. The first one is included as an example.

a. Inventory was received but not paid for on a purchase order. Payment terms were 2% 10 Net 30.

Account Number

DR   *12100 - Inventory Asset*

DR

CR   *20000 - Accounts Payable*

CR

b. A purchase order for the purchase of inventory was prepared and saved.

Account Number

DR   _____

DR   _____

CR   _____

CR   _____

c. The inventory received on a purchase order was paid for within 20 days of the purchase.

Account Number

DR   _____

DR   _____

CR   _____

CR   _____

d. An invoice was received and processed, but not paid for from Cal Gas & Electric.

Account Number

DR _____

DR _____

CR _____

CR _____

e. The invoice from Cal Gas & Electric was paid within 20 days of the purchase.

Account Number

DR _____

DR _____

CR _____

CR _____

f. The monthly payment to Bank of Anycity for its notes payable was paid.

Account Number

DR _____

DR _____

CR _____

CR _____

g. The invoice for accounting and tax services from Fay, Maureen Lynn, CPA was received and paid for.

Account Number

DR _____

DR _____

CR _____

CR _____

PROBLEM 6-9. Rock Castle Construction — Subsidiary account balances affected by processing purchasing and cash disbursement transactions

For each of the following transactions from Problem 6-8, state the subsidiary record or records affected by the transaction and show whether the effect on each was an increase or decrease by circling the correct change. The first one is included as an example.

a. Inventory was received but not paid for on a purchase order. Payment terms were 2% 10 Net 30.

		Account		
Subsidiary record	*Inventory*	(Increase)	Decrease
Subsidiary record	*Accounts Payable*	(Increase)	Decrease

b. A purchase order for the purchase of inventory was prepared and saved.

		Account		
Subsidiary record	_____	Increase	Decrease
Subsidiary record	_____	Increase	Decrease

c. The inventory received on a purchase order was paid for within 20 days of the purchase.

		Account		
Subsidiary record	_____	Increase	Decrease
Subsidiary record	_____	Increase	Decrease

d. An invoice was received and processed, but not paid for from Cal Gas & Electric.

		Account		
Subsidiary record	_____	Increase	Decrease
Subsidiary record	_____	Increase	Decrease

e. The invoice from Cal Gas & Electric was paid within 20 days of the purchase.

		Account		
Subsidiary record	_____	Increase	Decrease
Subsidiary record	_____	Increase	Decrease

f. The monthly payment to Bank of Anycity for its notes payable was paid.

Account

Subsidiary record	_____	Increase	Decrease
Subsidiary record	_____	Increase	Decrease

g. The invoice for accounting and tax services from Fay, Maureen Lynn, CPA was received and paid for.

Account

Subsidiary record	_____	Increase	Decrease
Subsidiary record	_____	Increase	Decrease

PROBLEM 6-10. Rock Castle Construction — Internal control questions

Required

a. Identify vendors' names that cannot be deleted on 12/15/2016. Why will *QuickBooks* not allow you to delete the accounts?

_____

_____

_____

b. Gregg Schneider is responsible for processing all purchase invoices. Explain why he is likely to need access to accounts payable maintenance. Explain why it is desirable to deny access to him for processing cash disbursement transactions.

_____

_____

_____

_____

_____

c. Gregg Schneider has accessed the Enter Bills window to process a purchase transaction for Daigle Lighting. List six types of information that can be accessed in the window by clicking on an icon or drop-down list arrow to reduce typing the information and thereby saving time and reducing the likelihood of errors:

1. Example: Vendor

2. _____

3. _____

4. _____

5. _____

6. _____

d. Gregg Schneider has entered all information needed to process a vendor's invoice for Daigle Lighting in the Enter Bills window and has clicked the Save and Close button to process the transaction. List six types of information that is automatically prepared or updated as a result of the activity:

1. Example: Vendor Balance; total list in the Vendor Center for Daigle Lighting is updated.

2. _____
_____

3. _____
_____

4. _____
_____

5. _____
_____

6. _____
_____

Name:

e. Gregg Schneider has accessed the Enter Bills window to process a purchase transaction for Daigle Lighting. List three pieces of information that are automatically displayed after Gregg has clicked on Daigle Lighting in the Vendor box.

_____

_____

_____

_____

_____

_____

_____

PROBLEM 6-11. Larry's Landscaping & Garden Supply — Processing transactions

Required

The following are situations where an error or fraud has occurred. You are to recommend one or more internal controls to prevent or detect the error or fraud.

a. Shane Hamby processed a nonexistent purchase transaction payable to himself. He then processed a check to pay for the purchase and forged the controller's signature.

_____

_____

_____

_____

b. Duncan Fisher, the employee responsible for processing purchases, started a fictitious company and processed a purchase transaction for that company. The cash disbursements processor processed the check to pay the invoice and the controller signed the check and mailed it to the fictitious company.

_____

_____

_____

_____

c. When Duncan Fisher established a new vendor in Maintain Vendors he entered the wrong default account for inventory. Every inventory purchase transaction with that vendor was processed using that wrong account.

_____

_____

_____

_____

PROBLEM 6-12. Larry's Landscaping & Garden Supply — Processing transactions

You are to do the maintenance and process the transactions that follow in the purchases and cash disbursements cycle for Larry's Landscaping & Garden Supply. The company has decided to add a limited line of outdoor furniture to their inventory to sell as retail to existing customers. They will start by buying two inventory items for resale: umbrellas and deck chairs.

a. First you will do the required maintenance.

⟳ *Do the maintenance required to set up the two inventory items using the information that follows.*

> **Information about the two inventory items**
>
> | | Umbrella | Deck Chair |
> |---|---|---|
> | **Type:** | Inventory Part | Inventory Part |
> | **Type Name:** | Umbrella | Deck Chair |
> | **Description:** | Umbrella | Deck Chair |
> | **Cost:** | $225.00 | $82.00 |
> | **Sales Price:** | $315.00 | $113.00 |
> | **COGS Account:** | Cost of Goods Sold | Cost of Goods Sold |
> | **Tax Code:** | Tax | Tax |
> | **Preferred Vendor:** | Conner Garden Supplies | Conner Garden Supplies |
> | **Income Account:** | Retail Sales | Retail Sales |
> | **Asset Account:** | Inventory Asset | Inventory Asset |
> | **Reorder Point:** | 20 | 50 |

b. A purchase order was sent to Conner Garden Supplies for the purchase of umbrellas and deck chairs. Information about the purchase order and inventory follows.

⟳ *Process the purchase order using the information that follows, print it, and save it.*

> | | |
> |---|---|
> | **Vendor:** | Conner Garden Supplies |
> | **Date:** | December 17, 2016 |
> | **PO Number:** | 6238 |
> | **Inventory items ordered:** | |
>
> | Qty. | Item | Description | Quantity | Unit Cost |
> |---|---|---|---|---|
> | 25 | Umbrella | Umbrella | 25 | $225.00 |
> | 40 | Deck Chair | Deck Chair | 40 | 82.00 |

c. The umbrellas and deck chairs ordered on Purchase Order No. 6238 were delivered December 19, 2016. Conner Garden Supplies delivered all of the umbrellas, but only 20 chairs. They included Invoice No. 4134 in the amount of $7,265.00. No payment was made.

Required

⟳ *Process the receipt of the inventory using the information provided and save the transaction.*

d. On December 26, 2016, Larry's Landscaping & Garden Supply paid for the full amount due on Invoice No. 4134 to Conner Garden Supplies.

Required

✧ *Process the payment of the invoice using the information provided. Before you save the information, write below the account numbers and amounts for the debits and credits.*

_____

_____

_____

_____

_____

✧ *Print the check and also save the information.*

e. On December 28, 2016, Larry's Landscaping & Garden Supply determined that 10 of the umbrellas on Invoice No. 4134 were not of the quality that had been agreed upon. Conner Garden Supplies agreed to pick the umbrellas up and give Larry's Landscaping & Garden Supply full credit. Conner Garden Supplies issued Credit Memo No. 72191 (processed as a debit memo by Larry's Landscaping & Garden Supply) on December 28, 2016, for the return.

Required

✧ *Process the debit memo (vendor credit memo) using the information provided. After you save the debit memo, write below the account numbers and amounts for the debits and credits.*

_____

_____

_____

_____

_____

Name:

Problems Dealing With the Sales and Cash Receipts Cycle

As described on page v of this book, you should restore both Rock Castle Construction and Larry's Landscaping & Garden Supply using the initial backups you copied to your hard drive while completing Chapter 1. Restore both companies before working on this chapter's problem material.

PROBLEM 7-1. Larry's Landscaping & Garden Supply — Credit Sales

Required

a. How many credit sales invoices have been processed so far in this fiscal quarter-to-date (10/01/2016 to 12/15/2016)? Do not include items with "FC" in the Num column; those are finance charges. *Note:* All parts of this problem relate to the current fiscal quarter-to-date.

b. What are the amounts of the two largest invoices?

c. What was sold on the second to the largest invoice?

d. What was the nature of the service provided to Ecker Design on Invoice No. 93?

e. What are the amounts of the two smallest invoices, ignoring finance charges (finance charges have FC prefixes)?

---

f. What is the lowest invoice number?

---

g. What is the accounting entry for a sale of inventory on credit?

---

h. Which subsidiary account/accounts is/are affected by sale of inventory on credit and how is each affected?

PROBLEM 7-2. Rock Castle Construction — Collection of Accounts Receivable

Required

a. How many sales invoices were collected using a customer's credit card in this fiscal year-to-date?

b. What are the amounts of the two largest cash receipts for this fiscal year-to-date?

c. For Receipt No. 41022 on 10/30/2016, what was the amount of the sales tax on the original invoice(s)?

d. How much was still due to Rock Castle Construction on Invoice No. 1072 after the payment of $10,000 by Brian Cook on Cash Receipt No. 9865?

e. Prepare a printout of all collections of accounts receivable for this fiscal year-to-date in excess of $5,000 sorted by last name from A to the last letter. The printout should include from left to right the date, customer, and the amount of collection. The printout should include proper headings and your name.

f. Which subsidiary account or accounts are affected when accounts receivable are collected?

Name:

PROBLEM 7-3. Rock Castle Construction — Accounts Receivable

Required

    a. What was the total of accounts receivable with balances outstanding in the 1–30 day category on November 30, 2016?

    b. What is the name of the customer with the largest receivables balance at 11/30/2016?

    c. How many customers are included in the Rock Castle Construction master file with a balance outstanding in excess of $5,000 at 11/30/2016?

    d. What are the company name, payment terms, and sales tax item for Johnny Melton?

Name:

PROBLEM 7-4. Larry's Landscaping & Garden Supply — Sales

The management of Larry's Landscaping & Garden Supply wants listings of sales invoices for the most recent quarter to date in 2016 (10/01/2016 to 12/15/16). The listing is to be sorted by sales invoice total from largest to smallest amount and is to include only the following six columns in the order listed, from left to right: customer, invoice number, invoice amount, invoice date, due date, and terms. Do not export to Excel. *Hint:* Use Customize Transaction List Columns.

Required

a. Prepare and print a list of the sales invoices in the format requested by management.

b. Why are the terms for several customers not included in the Terms column?

Note: In each case the invoice showed a due date the same as the invoice date.

_____

_____

_____

PROBLEM 7-5. Larry's Landscaping & Garden Supply — Collections on Accounts Receivable

The management of Larry's Landscaping & Garden Supply wants a listing of cash receipts from collections on accounts receivable in excess of $1,000 for this fiscal year-to-date (10/01/2016 to 12/15/2016). The listing is to be sorted by invoice date from earliest to latest and is to include only the following three columns in the order listed, from left to right: customer, collection amount, and collection date. The total of collections on the listing should be included. The schedule should have proper headings and your name. Export the information to Excel to complete the requirement.

Required

Prepare and print a list of the cash receipts from collections on accounts receivable in the format requested by management.

PROBLEM 7-6. Rock Castle Construction — Customer Statements

The management of Rock Castle Construction wants customer statements prepared and printed for three customers at November 30, 2016 (Robert Allard, Jason Burch, and Anton Teschner). The statement period should be from October 1, 2016, to November 30, 2016.

Required

a. Set the defaults for preparing statements using the criteria requested by management.

b. Print the customer statements.

PROBLEM 7-7. Rock Castle Construction — Customer Collections

The management of Rock Castle Construction wants an analysis of the Brian Cook customer account at year-end. Identify which sales invoices are still unpaid as of year-end.

Required

Prepare a report of these invoices with the following columns in the heading from left to right: Date, Invoice Number, Invoice Amount, and Amount Unpaid. Include a total of the amount unpaid and a heading showing your name and the name of the customer.

PROBLEM 7-8. Rock Castle Construction — Cash Sales

a. How many cash sales were processed for the year through December 31, 2016?

_____

b. What was sold on the largest cash sale for the entire year?

_____

c. Why was there no sales tax on the transaction in Problem 7-8b?

_____

_____

Name:

d. Four of the cash sale transactions had no Pay Method included in the Sales Receipts listing. Can you determine the payment method for these four cash sales and why the Pay Method wasn't indicated?

_____

_____

_____

_____

_____

_____

_____

e. What was the accounting entry for the 5/21/2016 cash sale to Reyes Properties on Invoice No. 3001, including the amounts? *Hint:* Use the Journal button.

_____

_____

_____

_____

_____

f. What subsidiary accounts were affected?

_____

_____

_____

_____

_____

Name:

PROBLEM 7-9. Rock Castle Construction — Sale of Inventory and Collection

A customer orders goods from Rock Castle Construction to be shipped in three days. The company completes all of the processes needed to ship the goods and bills customer. Later a portion of the goods are returned, and still later the Company collects the money owed on the sale. At each step the accountant prints the relevant document. List below the Home Page icon used to access the appropriate window for the sale, return, and collection; the document printed for each; the transaction listing in the Customer Center affected; and the master file or files affected.

Credit Sale:

Home Page Window Icon _____

Document Accessed _____

Transaction Printed _____

Listing Affected _____

Master file(s) Affected _____

_____

Return of Goods:

Home Page Window Icon _____

Document Accessed _____

Transaction Printed _____

Listing Affected _____

Master file(s) Affected _____

_____

Collection:

Home Page Window Icon _____

Document Accessed _____

Transaction Printed _____

Listing Affected _____

Master file(s) Affected _____

_____

Name:

PROBLEM 7-10. Rock Castle Construction — Credit Memos

a. How many credit memos were processed for the year through December 15, 2013?

_____

b. What was the nature of Credit Memo No. 4002?

_____

_____

c. What was the check number and amount of the check issued for the refund on the credit memo? *Hint:* Use the Transaction tab on the right side of the Create Credit Memos/Refunds window to locate the information.

_____

_____

d. Explain why Rock Castle Construction paid for the credit memo instead of crediting the customer's account balance.

_____

_____

_____

_____

_____

_____

Name:

PROBLEM 7-11. Rock Castle Construction — Internal Control

Required

a. Attempt to delete the accounts receivable Room Addition account for Jason Burch (Delete Customer: Job). What is the message on the window after you answer that you want to delete it? Why does that control exist?

_____

_____

_____

_____

_____

b. Elizabeth Mason is responsible for processing all sales invoices. Explain why she is likely to need access to accounts receivable maintenance.

_____

_____

_____

_____

c. Explain why it is desirable to deny Elizabeth access to processing cash receipt transactions, processing credit memos, and processing general journal transactions.

_____

_____

_____

_____

Name:

d. Elizabeth Mason has entered all information needed to process a sales invoice for Heather Campbell and has clicked the Save button in the Create Invoices–Accounts Receivable window. List seven types of information that are automatically prepared or updated as a result of the activity.

Note: There are many items in reports including those in Company & Financial, Customers & Receivables, Sales, and Accountant & Taxes.

1.   **Example:** Customer Balance—detail file for Heather Campbell
              is updated

2.   _____

3.   _____

4.   _____

5.   _____

6.   _____

7.   _____

e. Elizabeth Mason has accessed the Create Invoices–Accounts Receivable window to process a sales invoice for Aaron Davies. List six types of information that can be accessed in the window by clicking on an icon or drop-down arrow to reduce typing the information and thereby saving time and reducing the likelihood of errors.

1.   **Example:** Customer: Job

2.   _____

3.   _____

4.   _____

5.   _____

6.   _____

Name:

Problems Dealing With the Payroll Cycle and Other Activities

As described on page v of this book, you should restore both Rock Castle Construction and Larry's Landscaping & Garden Supply using the initial backups you copied to your hard drive while completing Chapter 1. Restore both companies before working on this chapter's problem material.

PROBLEM 8-1. Rock Castle Construction — Employees

Required

a. How many employees does Rock Castle Construction currently have on its master file? How often are employees paid?

b. What date was Dan Miller hired?

c. What is Miller's phone number?

d. What is the difference in the Company Summary and the Employee Summary boxes in the Review Paycheck window?

PROBLEM 8-2. Rock Castle Construction — Payroll

Required

a. Explain the difference between the following three reports:
   Payroll Summary, Payroll Item Detail, and Payroll Transaction Detail.

_____

_____

_____

_____

_____

_____

_____

_____

_____

_____

b. For the employee Elizabeth Mason, what are the total payroll amounts
   for 2016 to date for the following:

   ▧ Gross payroll _____

   ▧ Federal withholding _____

   ▧ California withholding _____

   ▧ Net pay _____

Name: _____

PROBLEM 8-3. Rock Castle Construction — Monthly payroll summary

Required

Summarize monthly payroll for each month listed below in 2016 for Gregg Schneider with the following information.

◻ **January**

Regular Hours: _____

Overtime Hours: _____

Gross Pay: _____

Net Pay: _____

◻ **February**

Regular Hours: _____

Overtime Hours: _____

Gross Pay: _____

Net Pay: _____

◻ **March**

Regular Hours: _____

Overtime Hours: _____

Gross Pay: _____

Net Pay: _____

Name:

PROBLEM 8-4. Larry's Landscaping & Garden Supply — Payroll Maintenance

a. Perform maintenance for a new hourly employee, Claire Woods, that Larry's Landscaping & Garden Supply hired on 12/23/2016 using the information that follows.

Personal Info (Change tabs)

Personal tab

■ **Name:**   Claire Woods

■ **Social Security Number:**   464-33-6430

Address and Contact tab

■ **Address:**   535 W. Spalding
     Bayshore, CA 94326

■ **Telephone:**   555-2039

Payroll and Compensation Info (Change tabs)

■ **Regular Pay:** $22 per hour

■ **Overtime Rate:** $33 per hour

■ **Pay Frequency:**   Bi-weekly

■ **Class:**   Maintenance

■ **Health Insurance Amount:**   – $62.75

Taxes button

Federal tab

■ **Filing Status:**   Single

■ **Allowances:**   2

State tab

■ **State:**   CA

■ **Allowances:**   2

Employment Info (Change tabs)

■ **Hire Date:**   12/23/2016

■ **Employment Details Type:**   Regular

---

b. Duncan Fisher has requested that his federal withholdings allowances be increased to 4, with no change in the others. Jenny Miller is now married and has changed her name to Jenny Albright. She has also requested a change in her filing status as of this pay period from single to married, and her allowance to 3 for all withholdings. Make these changes.

PROBLEM 8-5. Larry's Landscaping & Garden Supply — General journal entries

Required

a. What are the types of general journal entries that Larry's Landscaping & Garden Supply has made from this fiscal year to date?

_____

_____

_____

b. How often does Larry's Landscaping & Garden Supply record depreciation expense? *Hint:* Examine the general journal entries for the last fiscal year.

_____

PROBLEM 8-6. Rock Castle Construction — General journal entry for Allowance for uncollectible accounts

Rock Castle Construction management has never had an allowance for uncollectible accounts. Management decided to establish an allowance for uncollectible accounts at the beginning of the current fiscal year, 10/01/2016. Management decided on an allowance of $3,000 and they suggest 11500 as the account number.

Required

a. What is an explanation for why Rock Castle Construction did not previously have an allowance for uncollectible accounts?

_____

_____

_____

_____

b. Set up the allowance as of 10/01/2016. Management has decided to charge bad debt as the offset to the allowance. What were the accounts and subsidiary accounts, if any, that were affected?

c. At 12/15/2016, management decided to charge-off the entire remaining receivable from David Vitton. Make the accounting entry to charge-off the balance in the account. What were the accounts and subsidiary accounts, if any, that were affected?

d. On 12/31/2016, management reevaluates the allowance account and decides that the balance should now be $4,000. Make the adjustment.

e. What were the accounts and subsidiary accounts, if any, that were affected?

Name:

PROBLEM 8-7. Rock Castle Construction — Possible general journal entries

Required

A new accountant prepared the following general journal entries on February 28, 2016, for Rock Castle Construction. Each of these general journal entries includes an error. Describe the error.

1.

60600	Bank Service Charges	$ 112	
10100	Checking		$ 121
	Bank service charge for February		

2.

12000	Inventory	$5,279	
10100	Checking		$5,279
	Purchase of inventory		

3.

17000	Accumulated Depreciation	$1,500	
60900	Depreciation Expense		$1,500
	Depreciation for February		

Name:

4.

11500	Allowance for Uncollectible Accounts*	$ 450	
11000	Accounts Receivable		$ 450
	Charge-off an uncollectible account		

* This account was set up during the requirements for Problem 8-6.
If you did not complete Problem 8-6, just assume that the company's
accountant added the allowance account to the chart of accounts.

5.

50100	Cost of Goods Sold	$5,227	
12100	Inventory		$5,227
	Adjust inventory for differences between the master files and the actual inventory		

PROBLEM 8-8. Larry's Landscaping & Garden Supply — Inventory maintenance

The management of Larry's Landscaping & Garden Supply has decided
to discontinue providing the non-inventory item rock fountains and has
requested that all maintenance dealing with "rock fountains" be deleted.
They have also decided to increase the selling price of all service, inventory,
and non-inventory items that have a selling price of more than $30 and less
than $60 by $5.

Required

a. Try to delete the inventory account as instructed by management.
Why can't you? When will you be able to delete the item?

Name: _____

b. Change the price of the items as instructed by management and print an item price list report that reflects the changes.

c. What will you do with a deleted inventory or non-inventory item if management later decides to begin providing rock fountains again?

_____

_____

_____

PROBLEM 8-9. Larry's Landscaping & Garden Supply — Adjusting inventory

There have been minimal sales of both rock fountains and fountain pumps this fiscal year. Rock fountains are not carried in inventory, but the quantity in the master file for fountain pumps is overstated. Management believes that there have been thefts and therefore requested that a count be made at 11/30/2016. The count showed 20 in current inventory. Management requests that a new account be set up for any necessary adjustment to the expense account "Inventory Shortage." Set the new account up "on the fly."

Required

a. Adjust the perpetual records of inventory to reflect the actual count, following management's instructions.

b. Print the Item List. Include only the following three columns in the order listed from left to right: description, standard (selling price), and quantity on hand. The report should include the company name, a description of the report, date, column headings, and the information requested.

c. Print a standard income statement for October 1 to November 30, 2016.

d. Suggest an internal control to reduce the likelihood of theft of the inventory.

_____

_____

_____

Name:

PROBLEM 8-10. Rock Castle Construction — Inventory dollar balances

QuickBooks maintains balances of inventory quantities in the inventory Item List, but not dollar amounts. Management wants to be sure the quantities in the Item List are consistent with the general ledger if the inventory items were extended.

Required

a. Use a different method to determine the total cost of each item in inventory and the total cost of all inventory items included in the inventory master file at 11/30/2016.

b. Compare the cost you arrived at in Problem 8-10a to the balance in the general ledger at 11/30/2016. What are the respective amounts? Which amount is correct?

_____

_____

_____

_____

_____

_____

_____

PROBLEM 8-11. Larry's Landscaping & Garden Supply — Bank reconciliation questions

Required

a. What is the purpose of bank reconciliation?

_____

_____

_____

b. How many bank reconciliations will be made each month for Larry's Landscaping & Garden Supply if they are done monthly?

_____

c. For good internal control, how often should bank reconciliations be prepared?

_____

_____

_____

PROBLEM 8-12. Rock Castle Construction — Bank reconciliation problem

Management requests that you prepare a bank reconciliation of the regular bank account as of November 30, 2016, for Rock Castle Construction. The following information is provided for the bank reconciliation. Recall that at the beginning of the problem material in this chapter, you were reminded to restore the Rock Castle Construction dataset using the initial backup you made in Chapter 1. This problem assumes you have restored the initial backup, so if you have not done that yet you should do it now.

Balance per bank statement 11/30/2016:		$58,860.89
Outstanding checks as of 11/30/2016:		

Check No.	Amount
466	$ 600.00
468	6,790.00

Deposit in Transit:	$4,135.50
February bank service charge already debited to account by bank (A/C No. 60600):	$35.00

Required

a. Prepare a bank reconciliation as of November 30 for the regular checking account using the preceding information.

b. Print and hand in the reconciliation after you have completed it.

Questions About Waren Sports Supply

Accrued Interest Payable

Interest accruals are calculated using a 365-day year with the day after the note was made counting as the first day. General ledger account numbers for the journal entry are: A/C #40800 (Interest Expense) and A/C #20900 (Interest Payable). Show your calculation below.

Bad Debt Expense and Allowance

Bad debt expense is estimated once annually at the end of each year as 1/4 of one percent (0.0025) of net sales and is recorded in the general journal as of December 31. The "allowance" method of recording bad debt expense is used. General ledger account numbers for the journal entry are: A/C #40900 (Bad Debt Expense) and A/C #10300 (Allowance for Doubtful Account). Show your calculation below.

Federal Income Taxes

Corporate income tax rates for 2013 are: 15% of the first $50,000 of pre-tax income, plus 25% of the next $25,000, plus 36% of all pre-tax income over $75,000. General ledger account numbers for the journal entry are: A/C #40700 (Federal Income Tax Expense) and A/C #20700 (Federal Income Taxes Payable). Show your calculation below.

Name:

Problems Dealing With New Company Setup

As described on page v of this book, you should restore both Rock Castle Construction and Larry's Landscaping & Garden Supply using the initial backups you copied to your hard drive while completing Chapter 1. Restore both companies before working on this chapter's problem material.

PROBLEM 10-1. Larry's Landscaping & Garden Supply — Setup of company information

Required

a. What is the Federal Employer ID for Larry's Landscaping & Garden Supply and how was it entered into *QuickBooks*? *Hint:* Start with the Menu Bar to find the information.

b. If you decided to change that information, how would you change it?

PROBLEM 10-2. Larry's Landscaping & Garden Supply — Setup

Assume Larry's Landscaping & Garden Supply converted from a manual system to *QuickBooks*.

Required

a. How many times did Larry's Landscaping & Garden Supply likely use the *QuickBooks* setup procedures?

_____

b. What are the likely similarities and differences in what you did in setup and what Larry's Landscaping & Garden Supply personnel did in their conversion from a manual system to *QuickBooks*?

_____

_____

_____

_____

_____

c. Why is it likely that it took Larry's Landscaping & Garden Supply personnel considerably longer to make the conversion to *QuickBooks* than it took you in this project?

_____

_____

_____

_____

_____

d. Why was the Larry's Landscaping & Garden Supply conversion from a manual system to *QuickBooks* most likely done at a year-end instead of during the year?

_____

_____

_____

_____

e. Assume management decided to convert from a manual system to *QuickBooks* halfway through a year. Describe the process as to how the conversion would likely occur.

_____

_____

_____

_____

PROBLEM 10-3. Rock Castle Construction — Changing information for a vendor

Required

Assume you entered the wrong address information for a vendor and did not discover it until after you had completed all setup procedures. How would you correct the vendor's address?

_____

_____

_____

Name:

PROBLEM 10-4. Larry's Landscaping & Garden Supply — Accounts receivable setup

You entered all information in *QuickBooks* during setup in a conversion from a manual system to *QuickBooks*, including the transactions that make up the beginning balance in accounts receivable. The debits and credits in the ending balance in the general ledger trial balance are equal. When you compare the accounts receivable total in the general ledger trial balance to the balance in manual system, there is a $4,000 difference. Your assistant suggests that you should make a general journal entry to correct the difference.

Required

a. Can you now change the total in the *QuickBooks* general ledger trial balance to make it equal the balance in the manual system?

_____

_____

b. How can you determine if the difference results from an error in the manual system or the information you entered in *QuickBooks*?

_____

_____

c. If there is an error in the *QuickBooks* accounts receivable balance, what likely caused the error?

_____

_____

d. Explain how you will correct the error if there is one.

_____

_____

_____

_____

Name:

PROBLEM 10-5. Change from a system using *Peachtree* to *QuickBooks*

Ablon, Inc. used *Peachtree* software for several years and decided to switch to *QuickBooks* at 1/1/2013. Ablon's has 35 employees, 500 customers, 250 vendors, and 300 inventory items.

Required

a. What are the similarities and differences in the conversion from *Peachtree* to *QuickBooks* compared to a conversion from a manual system?

_____

_____

_____

_____

_____

_____

b. Why would the conversion from a manual system be extremely time consuming whereas the conversion from *Peachtree* to *QuickBooks* could be done fairly quickly?

_____

_____

_____

_____

_____

_____